HABITATS
Tropical Grasslands

Robert Snedden

FRANKLIN WATTS
LONDON • SYDNEY

An Appleseed Editions book

First published in 2004 by Franklin Watts
96 Leonard Street, London, EC2A 4XD

Franklin Watts Australia
45–51 Huntley Street, Alexandria, NSW 2015

Created by Appleseed Editions Ltd,
Well House, Friars Hill, Guestling, East Sussex, TN35 4ET

Designed by Helen James

ISBN 0 7496 5718 9

A CIP catalogue for this book is available from the British Library.

Photographs by Corbis (AFP, O. Alamany & E. Vicens, Theo Allofs, Yann Arthus-Bertrand, Bernard and Catherine Desjeux, Gallo Images, Martin Harvey, Peter Johnson, Wolfgang Kaehler, Otto Lang, Craig Lovell, William Manning, Chris Mattison; Frank Lane Picture Agency, Mary Ann McDonald, Sally A. Morgan; Ecoscene, NASA, Rod Patterson; Gallo Images, Carl & Ann Purcell, Steve Reynolds and the FAO Grassland Index, D. Robert & Lorri Franz, Galen Rowell, David Turnley, Brian A. Vilkander, Michael S. Yamashita)

Printed and bound in the USA

Contents

An ocean of grass   4

The monsoon zone   6

Soil and grasses   8

Grass fires   10

Animals of the grasslands   12

Grassland birds   14

The wandering wildebeest   16

Grassland leapers   18

Pride of the grasslands   20

Running with the pack   22

Ants and acacias   24

Kopje communities   26

Grasslands under threat   28

Glossary   30

Index   32

An ocean of grass

Tropical grasslands, also called savannas, grow between tropical rainforests and deserts. They develop where the weather is not wet enough for a forest to grow and not dry enough for a desert to form. Tropical grasslands cover a huge area of the Earth's surface. Half of Africa is grassland, as are large areas of South America, India and Australia.

Tropical grasslands are mostly made up of grasses. This does not mean that there are no trees at all. Scattered trees grow across the savanna, but there are few trees in true grasslands, for several reasons. The **climate** may be too dry, the soils may be too poor, or frequent fires prevent tree seedlings from growing. The trees that do grow on the savanna have **adapted** to the conditions there.

The most interesting of the tropical grassland **biomes** are the savannas of Africa. Here there is an enormous number of animals which are adapted

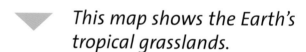

This map shows the Earth's tropical grasslands.

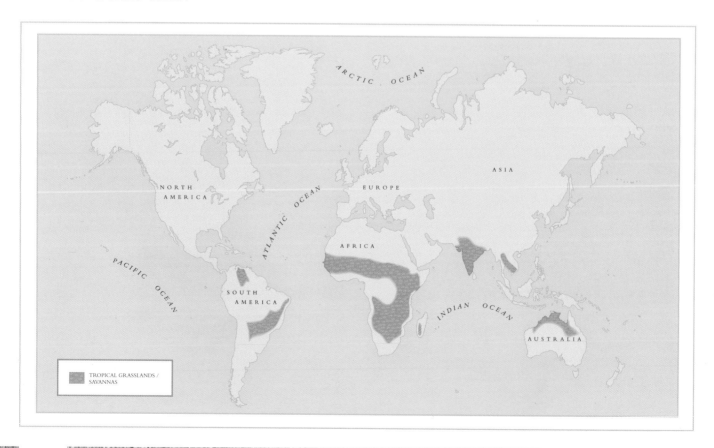

TROPICAL GRASSLANDS / SAVANNAS

Dry conditions and poor soil stop trees growing on the savanna.

solely to grassland life – more animals than anywhere else in the world. In South America, the wildlife of the tropical grasslands is usually found in other habitats as well. Few animals, if any, live on the grasslands and nowhere else. This book concentrates on life on the African savanna.

Creating grasslands

A number of factors create a grassland. Climate is one factor, but there are a number of other forces at work, too. Savannas grow where people have cleared forest land for farming. Once the land has been abandoned, some trees may return, but grasses usually take over the bare ground. In Africa, if too many elephants gather in one place, they can create savanna by destroying trees as they search for food. The grasslands around the Orinoco River in Venezuela and Columbia, called the llanos, are maintained by the annual flooding of the river. Grasses can tolerate the wet conditions, but most trees will not grow on the flooded land. Fire is a major factor in preventing trees from growing in the savanna. The savannas of southeast Asia are generally considered to be almost entirely the result of humans who have started fires.

The monsoon zone

Climate affects where savannas will grow. Savannas have high average annual temperatures and a great deal of rain. However, it does not rain all the year round in the grasslands.

In the savanna the weather is rainy for six to eight months at a time. For the rest of the year, it is dry. This is called the tropical wet and dry climate zone, or **monsoon** zone.

The dry season

A series of violent thunderstorms in October, followed by a strong, drying wind, signals the beginning of the dry season. During the dry season, rivers and streams dry up. Animals have difficulty finding enough to drink, and many plants shrivel and die. Most of the animals **migrate** long distances in their search for water. Between December and February, there is likely to be no rain at all.

Life becomes harder for plants and animals as the dry season progresses.

The torrential rain of the wet season quickly fills dried-up riverbeds.

The rainy season

In March, violent thunderstorms return to the savanna. This time they mark the start of the rainy season. The wet season is often called the monsoon. A great deal of rain falls and the days are very hot and **humid**. Warm, moist air rises up from the ground. As soon as it hits colder air higher up, it turns into rain and falls back to the Earth. Often the rain pours without stopping for hours on end. An average of between 75 and 100 centimetres of rain falls on the savanna over a year, almost all of it during the monsoon season.

When the rains come, everything changes. The savanna grasses grow rapidly. Some grasses can grow 2.5 centimetres or more in a single day. More grass means more food for the savanna animals to eat. Plant-eating animals, or **herbivores**, time the birth of their young to match the new plant growth. Females can produce plenty of milk for their young with so much grass to eat.

CONSTANT WARMTH

The temperature of the tropical grasslands does not change much over the course of the year. The dry season is cooler than the wet season but only by a few degrees. During the winter, the temperature ranges from about 20-25° Celsius. In the summer, the range is from 25-30° Celsius.

Carnivores, the animals which hunt the plant-eaters, have their young at this time of year too.

Soil and grasses

The layer of soil that provides growing plants with **nutrients** is called humus. Humus is made up of the decaying remains of plant and animal waste. In the dusty, red savanna soil, this layer may be very thin. Water drains rapidly through the savanna's **porous** soil.

These conditions mean that the plants that grow there have to be able to take up nutrients quickly and efficiently. They must also be able to grow in dry conditions.

Food supply

Most of the plants on the tropical grasslands are grasses, but there are often flowering plants, such as lilies, orchids and gladioli, growing among them. The grasses are the basic food supply for the savanna's plant-eating animals. The important thing about grasses is that they keep growing, no matter how much they are nibbled. They can do this because they grow from the base of their leaves, down near the soil. As long as any green part remains

Savanna grasses can withstand intense grazing by plant-eating animals such as this Thomson's gazelle.

Rhodes grass is a typical savanna grass that spreads quickly by producing trailing stems, or runners.

above the ground, the grass will grow. In ideal conditions, grasses grow rapidly.

Savanna grasses often reach heights of between 1.8 and 3 metres. Because the grasses grow so well, the savanna produces enough food to support an incredible number of animals.

Underground stores

Grasses are also very good at surviving dry conditions. Their roots stay **dormant** beneath the ground during the dry season, then send up new shoots when the rains come. The grasses' deep roots are also protected from fire damage. About half of the total weight of a savanna's grasses is underground in the form of roots.

Different grasses grow in different savannas because the rainfall and soil vary from place to place. For example, Rhodes grass and red oat grass are common in drier savannas with well-drained soils, such as those on the Serengeti plains of Africa. In East Africa, star grasses are most abundant.

Grass fires

A raging fire burning unchecked across the grasslands seems disastrous. However, the fires that sweep the savanna during the long dry season are very important in maintaining this biome. Fires often happen around the height of the dry season, in January. They can be extremely hot, with flames leaping 12–15 metres into the air.

Every year, large areas of Australia's tropical grasslands are consumed by fire.

The damage caused by a wild grassland fire can be seen easily from space.

grasses are burned away, the deep roots remain unharmed. These roots generate new growth when moisture returns to the soil. Many grass **species** can grow back very quickly after a fire has swept through the grassland. Some grasses have seeds that **germinate** only after being burned in a fire.

Shrubs can also survive fires well, relying on the food reserves stored in their roots until they can regrow above ground. Some trees have a corky, fire-resistant bark that gives some protection. Small, young tree saplings do not have the reserves of moisture they need to survive. Fire is one reason more trees do not grow on the grasslands.

Very few large animals die in the fires, as they can usually outrun them. Most of the animals that are killed are insects. After the fires have died down, birds and other animals return to feed on the remains of the grasshoppers, beetles and other small creatures that were not swift enough to escape the flames.

Surviving the fire

Grasses can tolerate burning quite well, as their roots survive beneath the ground. Although the dry stems and leaves of the

MAN-MADE FIRES

Savanna fires are often deliberately set by **poachers** who want to clear away dead grass to make it easier to see the trophy animals they want to catch.

Animals of the grasslands

Savannas teem with animal life. On the grasslands of Africa, there are more than 40 different types of hoofed mammals alone, including a variety of antelopes such as the hartebeest, eland, impala, gazelle, oryx and kudu.

Herds of wildebeest, warthogs, water buffalo, zebras, giraffes, elephants and rhinoceroses all browse the plants of the savanna. There is little competition between these plant-eaters, as they each have their own preferred foods and times for eating. Zebras eat some of the tougher grasses, while hartebeest nibble the stalks of plants that have had their leaves stripped by previous **foragers**. Giraffes and elephants feed on trees and shrubs.

On the grasslands of Australia, herds of kangaroos and wallabies graze on the grasses. In South America, giant anteaters break open the nests of termites and ants. Capybaras, the world's largest rodents, and long-legged, hare-like maras are the most common of the South American plant-eaters.

Some savanna animals are very well adapted to the dry conditions which last

The dik dik is a small antelope about the size of a fox. It lives in the dry bushland on the edge of the savanna.

Termites are an important part of the grassland biome, as they recycle plant remains.

for half the year. Small antelopes such as the dik dik and gernuk need no water. They absorb all the moisture they need from their food.

A wide range of meat-eaters preys on the plant-eaters of the savanna. These animal hunters include jackals and wild dogs, hyenas and big cats, such as lions, leopards and cheetahs. Many of them make use of the tall grasses to **ambush** their **prey**.

Insects by the billion

Insects make up the largest group of animals on the savannas. Countless billions of locusts, termites and flies swarm there. Locusts form colossal swarms that strip the vegetation even faster than the herds of large herbivores can. Other insects, such as dung beetles, scurry around feeding on the huge quantities of droppings left by the browsing herds. Termites eat dead plant matter, and **recycle** its nutrients for reuse by new plant growth. They also turn over tonnes of soil. In doing so, the termites let air into the soil, bringing vital oxygen to the animals that live in the soil and to the roots of the plants growing there, which need it to survive.

Safety in numbers

Most of the plant-eating mammals of the open savanna are herd animals, including zebras, giraffes and gazelles. Living together in herds provides some protection from **predators**. It is better to have several sets of eyes, ears and noses on the alert for danger rather than just one. Herds are often organized into groups of females and their young, with perhaps a single dominant male and a few junior males.

Grassland birds

Grasslands are rich in seeds, insects and other food sources, which means that they can also support large numbers of birds.

Many savanna birds make their homes on the ground, either because they cannot fly or because trees suitable for nesting are rare. Among the most numerous are the seed-eating weavers. These birds are members of the sparrow family. They get their name from their ability to make nests by weaving strands of grass together like a basket. Some weavers build hundreds of nests in a single tree. The sociable weaver builds big nests for a large number of birds to use together. A single huge structure with many entrances and hundreds of nests inside is built by dozens of birds working together.

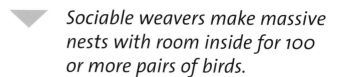

Sociable weavers make massive nests with room inside for 100 or more pairs of birds.

The secretary bird strides across the grasslands like someone on stilts.

Big birds

The grasslands are home to the world's biggest birds. South America has the rhea, Australia has the cassowary and the emu, and Africa has the ostrich. These birds are all rather similar in appearance. None of them can fly, but they can run swiftly across the grassland plains. They have long, powerful legs, long necks and big bodies. The ostrich is the world's biggest bird. An adult male may stand 2.7 metres tall.

Birds of prey

Tropical grasslands are an ideal hunting ground for many birds of prey. They soar effortlessly, held aloft by the warm air rising from the ground. One of the largest eagles in the world, the martial eagle, lives there. It swoops down to catch young antelope and ground birds such as the guinea fowl.

One of the more unusual birds of prey is the secretary bird. Its name comes from the tufts of feathers on its head that look like old-fashioned quill pens. It can fly but prefers not to. Instead it walks on the savanna on its long legs, looking for its favourite meals — snakes. If it finds one, it grabs the snake in its claws and beats it to death, using its big wings to protect itself from bites.

BIRDS BY THE BILLION

The most common wild bird on Earth is the red-billed quelea, a type of weaver which lives on the African savanna. There may be more than 10 billion of these birds in the world. Red-billed queleas love grass seeds and are serious pests on African farms, as they eat the seeds of cereal crops, as well as those of the wild savanna grasses.

The wandering wildebeest

The African savanna is home to enormous herds of wildebeest. The most common is the blue wildebeest, or brindled gnu.

The wildebeest is a large antelope with a slate-grey coat, a black tail, a narrow head and a long, flat face. It has short, curved horns and its eyes are set high and far apart on its head, giving it a puzzled expression. It also has a mane and a beard that hangs down the length of its neck. The wildebeest's front quarters are heavily built, its back slopes downwards and it balances on four thin legs. A full-grown wildebeest stands about 1.2 metres tall at the shoulder. Males weigh between 180 and 225 kilograms, and females weigh between 135 and 180 kilograms.

CLOWNS OF THE SAVANNA

The wildebeest's oddly shaped body and thin legs give it a rather strange running style. It has been described as jerking along like a wind-up toy. When wildebeest get excited, they often prance around in a manner that has earned them the title Clowns of the Veldt (veldt is a type of savanna).

A new-born wildebeest staggers to its feet. Soon it will join the safety of the herd.

Wildebeest migration

The movement of huge herds of wildebeest and other herbivores as they roam the grasslands of the Serengeti in Africa is a spectacular sight. A million and a half wildebeest, half a million gazelles and a quarter of a million zebras make the great migration in search of rainfall and the plant growth it brings. The wildebeest follow a great circular path, spending the wet season in the south-eastern Serengeti and the dry season in the woodlands to the north. The herd travels a total of more than 1,600 kilometres from grassland to woodland and back again.

Female wildebeest all give birth at more or less the same time between January and March, when the grass is at its best. On the plains it is easy to spot the approach of predators. Wildebeest calves are up and running very quickly after birth and soon join the safety of the herd.

Hundreds of thousands of wildebeest trek across the savanna in search of water and fresh grass.

DANGEROUS CROSSING

Wildebeest do not like crossing rivers, with good reason. Beneath the water big crocodiles lie in wait for the migrating herd, ready to snatch an unwary wildebeest as it wades to the other side.

Grassland leapers

There are no plant-eating animals with hoofs like the wildebeest in Australia. The role that is played by animals such as antelope, deer, cattle and sheep elsewhere in the natural world is played by kangaroos and wallabies in Australia.

Big feet

The scientific name for kangaroos and wallabies is macropods, which means big feet. They have powerful back legs that they use for hopping around. A big kangaroo can leap 6 metres or more in a single bound. Its large tail provides balance during leaps and is used as a prop to support the animal when it is standing still.

The macropod most often found on the grassy plains of Australia is the red kangaroo. This animal is well adapted to the dry conditions there, as it can live on very little water. The red kangaroo is also the biggest of the macropods. An adult male grows to about 1.5 metres tall at the shoulder. Grey kangaroos need more drinking water than reds and prefer to live in woodlands, but they come out on to the grasslands to graze at night when it is cool. Wallabies are very much like kangaroos in appearance, but smaller. There are about a dozen different kinds, or species, of wallabies, some of which live on the

A male kangaroo can travel at around 65 kilometres per hour.

grasslands. Kangaroos and wallabies eat grasses, leaves and roots. They prefer grass that is green and fresh.

This mob of kangaroos is peacefully grazing on the grasslands of Australia.

Kangaroo families

Kangaroos usually live in family groups called mobs. There can be as many as a hundred kangaroos in a mob. Male kangaroos are called boomers, females are called fliers, and the youngsters are called joeys. Some kangaroos act as lookouts for the rest of the mob while they feed. If there is any threat, they bang their tails on the ground and leap suddenly, alerting the mob to scatter.

Marsupials

Kangaroos and wallabies are part of the family of animals called **marsupials**. Unlike wildebeest calves, which are born ready to run, marsupial babies are very

small and helpless when they are born. A newborn grey kangaroo weighs just 0.8 grams. It crawls through its mother's fur to her pouch where it can feed on its mother's milk and continue growing.

ONE WAY ONLY

A big tail is useful for leaning on when you're standing still, but it does have one drawback: kangaroos can't move backwards.

Pride of the grasslands

The most powerful predator of the savanna is, without doubt, the lion. Lions are the only big cats which live in groups, called prides.

Lions can vary in colour from a dark yellow-brown to almost white. They are the only cats which have a tuft on the end of their tail. Male lions develop a thick, dark mane on their neck and shoulders as they reach adulthood. Again, they are the only cats to have a mane like this. The mane gives the lion an impressive appearance, earning it the title King of the Beasts.

A full-grown male lion can measure almost 1.8 metres long, stand a metre or more at the shoulder, and weigh more than 200 kilograms.

Pride life

Lions can adapt to a variety of **habitats**, but they most often live on the savanna. They are the most social of all cats. A pride of lions can number up to 30, including a dozen or so females and their young and about six adult males. Lionesses tend to stay in the pride in which they are born.

The magnificent mane and noble expression of the male lion have earned it the title King of the Beasts.

Cubs are cared for by all the females in the pride. Males are sent away from the pride when they reach adulthood and may form bands with other males. Living in a group increases the lions' chances of success in hunting and of defending their catch against other predators, such as hyenas. Hyenas are one of the few animals that attack lions. Injured lions may be killed by hyenas, and lions and hyenas often fight over prey.

Male lions defend the pride against intruders. Males fight fiercely with each other to become the head of a pride. Their mane gives them some protection, but serious, sometimes fatal, injuries often

Lions are the only cats that form family groups.

result from these battles. One of the first things a new male does is kill all the cubs in the pride. This means that only he will be the father of the pride's cubs.

Deadly females

Lions hunt by ambushing their prey, and females do most of the hunting. Their main prey includes medium- to large-sized animals such as wildebeest, other antelopes, zebras and warthogs. Smaller female lions chase their prey towards the biggest, strongest females, who lie hidden in the grasses, ready to pounce. Lions also **scavenge** for food and steal prey from other predators if they get the chance. Lions are well adapted to dry season life. They can survive for long periods without water, as they can absorb enough moisture from the meat of their prey.

Running with the pack

The African wild dog is one of the savanna's most **formidable** hunters. What it lacks in size, it makes up for in numbers. Working in packs, wild dogs can bring down bigger prey than a single dog could.

Wild dogs live mostly on the savanna of Africa, though they may also be found in open woodland. Their distinctive coats are a series of black, yellow and white blotches. Every animal has a distinctive set of markings, which may help other members of the pack identify it. African wild dogs are sometimes called painted wolves, and they are about the size of small wolves. They measure about a metre long, stand up to 75 centimetres at the shoulder, and weigh an average of 25 kilograms. They have extraordinarily big ears and a keen sense of hearing. Their long, slim legs are ideally suited to fast running.

Pack life

Each wild dog pack has a dominant (leading) male, who is the father of most of the pups, as well as a dominant female. All the members of the pack care for the pups.

Pups are born in a den, where they stay for the first three months of their lives. There are usually ten or eleven pups in a litter

Wild dogs have large litters. The whole pack helps to look after the growing pups.

Wild dogs do not hide from their prey. They rely on their speed and staying power to make a kill.

and sometimes as many as 20. It would be difficult, if not impossible, for one dog to look after so many pups alone. While the new mother is nursing, other members of the pack bring food to the den. Later, when the mother can leave the pups for a short time, other pack members act as babysitters, protecting the pups from any predators that wander too close to the den. A pack with fewer than four members rarely succeeds in raising any pups.

Tireless hunters

African wild dogs prey on grazing animals such as wildebeest, zebras and gazelles. The pack works together to catch animals that are much bigger than they are. Unlike lions, which also hunt together, wild dogs do not attempt to hide or to ambush their prey. The pack simply moves towards the herd it has targeted until the animals **stampede** in panic. The pack, led by the dominant male, then singles out an individual animal, usually one that is slower than the others because it is sick or old. The pack chases it until it drops from exhaustion. Wild dogs are swift and tireless, and can easily keep up a chase for an hour or more.

When the dogs return from a kill, they bring food to the young pups and to any wounded or sick dogs that were not able to go on the hunt.

Ants and acacias

One of the few trees dotting the flat landscape of the African savanna is the acacia, or whistling thorn. This tree has two defences against browsing animals. The first is a series of very sharp double thorns up to 8 centimetres long, and the second is its own army of biting ants.

Living together

Acacia trees are always occupied by ants. Some types of ants are found only in acacia trees. They live in the swollen bases of a tree's thorns and swarm out immediately if anything touches the tree, adding their stinging bites to the stabbing of the very sharp thorns. The ants eat a sugary sweet substance produced by special parts of the acacia tree's leaves called nectaries.

Angry ants

There are four different kinds of ants that make their homes in acacias, but only one kind lives there at a time.

Some acacia ants are very aggressive. At the slightest disturbance, they swarm out angrily to launch a biting attack. These ants are very effective at keeping away browsing animals.

A herd of elephants keeps cool in the shade of an acacia tree.

The black acacia ant is more timid. This ant uses the acacia's thorns as a hiding place, scurrying inside at any disturbance.

Some ants maintain herds of scale insects. These are major plant pests that feed on sap and damage the plant. The ants protect the scale insects and feed off the sweet substance they produce. The acacia tree gains no benefit from the insects that infest it.

Another type of ant damages the acacia tree. It nips off the flower buds and other growing tips of the tree with its powerful jaws. This makes the tree increase the size of the nectaries on its leaves, so the ants get more food. However, it harms the tree by preventing it from producing flowers and seeds.

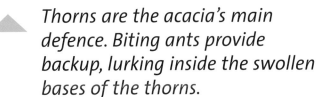

Thorns are the acacia's main defence. Biting ants provide backup, lurking inside the swollen bases of the thorns.

MINIATURE FLUTES

The swollen bases of acacia thorns are pierced by a number of tiny holes that serve as front doors for the ants. These holes also turn the thorns into miniature flutes, as they make a whistling noise when the wind blows across them. That's why acacias are also called whistling thorns.

Kopje communities

The flat expanse of the African savanna is broken here and there by mounds of rough and jumbled rock standing out from the plain. These are called inselbergs or kopjes and they are made of very old, hard-wearing granite.

The interesting thing about the kopjes is that they are habitat islands in the middle of the savanna with their own unique plants and wildlife. Kopjes are one of the few places where the grassland animals can take refuge from the heat of the sun.

Kopjes stand out like rocky islands in a sea of grass.

Hyraxes

One of the most common kopje inhabitants is the hyrax. Hyraxes are small animals, about the size of rabbits, with a rodent-like appearance. They have stocky bodies with thick brown fur, short sturdy legs and a stumpy tail. Their feet act like tiny suction cups, so the animals can hold on to the surface of their rocky homes. Hyraxes make their homes in holes in the rocks that are big enough for them but small

enough to keep out leopards and other predators.

Hyraxes are plant-eaters, browsing on the sparse vegetation of the kopje. Most **mammals** keep themselves warm by generating heat energy from the food they eat. Hyraxes, however, have adapted to life where food is scarce and not particularly nutritious. They make up for the lack of energy in their food by huddling together to keep warm at night and basking in the sun by day.

The tops of the kopjes make ideal nesting sites for large birds of prey such as eagles. Eagles often swoop down to catch unwary hyraxes, hares and even small antelopes. Among other hyrax predators are the cobras and adders that live in the rock crevices of the kopje.

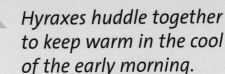

Hyraxes huddle together to keep warm in the cool of the early morning.

Mongooses and antelopes

Mongooses are often seen around kopjes. The slightly-built mongoose has a long face and body and a long bushy tail. It is very agile and active, feeding on a varied diet of such things as snakes, lizards, mice, birds' eggs, insects, fruit and berries.

Other inhabitants of the kopje include a type of antelope about the size of a goat called a klipspringer. Perched on the tips of their narrow hoofs, klipspringers leap with great agility from rock to rock of the kopje.

27

Grasslands under threat

Many people believe that the first humans came from the savanna grasslands of eastern and southern Africa. Many of the Earth's most important food grains, such as wheat, maize, barley, rice and millet, had their origins there, too. Today, the place that might have been the birthplace of humans is under threat.

The farming people of the savanna compete with wildlife for the resources of the grasslands.

Cattle versus wildlife

One of the most serious threats to the wildlife of the African savanna comes from people grazing cattle there. Some of the people of the savanna depend almost entirely on their cattle for their livelihood. This makes them reluctant to share the grasslands with animals that compete with their cattle for food. Farmers who use the grasslands in South America for cattle ranching and other agricultural purposes

have put wildlife there at risk. For example, numbers of the flightless rhea have fallen to dangerously low levels.

If just one type of animal grazes on the grasslands, this threatens the plants that grow there, too. Wild animals graze on a wide range of plants, including the more indigestible ones. Cattle, on the other hand, prefer the softer grasses and ignore the tougher, spinier plants. Eventually, the grasses disappear altogether.

Desertification

Farmers and their **domesticated** animals don't move around very much, unlike the wandering herds of wild animals. This means that the grasses in an area are soon eaten up, and the soil is broken down by the trampling hoofs of the animals. With no vegetation to hold it in place, the soil blows away, and the savanna turns into desert. This process is called **desertification**.

 In the Sahel region of Africa desert and grasslands meet. Today the desert is growing, while the grasslands are shrinking.

What can be done?

Providing money so that grassland areas can be set aside and protected may be one way to save them, but it would be hard to persuade African farmers to change their way of life. They need to feed their families, too. Climate change brought about by **global warming** is also likely to speed up the process of desertification. This can be prevented by carefully monitoring the use of **fossil fuels** such as coal and oil and finding cleaner energy alternatives. If people burn fewer fossil fuels, fewer **greenhouse gases** will be pumped into the air. These gases are believed to cause global warming. If people want to help save the world's biomes, their motto needs to be 'reduce, reuse and recycle'.

Glossary

adapted Suited to life in a particular environment.

ambush To hide, then attack by surprise.

biome Large areas of the environment with distinctive climates and plant types; examples include forests, mountains and deserts.

carnivores Animals that feed on other animals; meat-eaters.

climate The general weather conditions in a particular area.

desertification The changing of a habitat such as a grassland into a desert habitat as a result of climate change or human interference.

domesticated Describes an animal that has been tamed for use by humans, for work, food or companionship. Domestic means 'of the home'.

dormant In a state of inactivity before growth starts again. A seed can lie dormant in the ground until the conditions are right for growth.

foragers Searchers for food.

formidable Difficult to overcome.

fossil fuels Fuels such as coal, crude oil and natural gas that are formed from the remains of plants and animals that lived millions of years ago.

germinate To start to grow. When a seed grows and produces its first root and leaves, it has germinated.

global warming The increase in the average temperature of the Earth, thought to be the result of the increasing amount of greenhouse gases in the atmosphere.

greenhouse gases Gases in the atmosphere that trap heat as it rises from the surface of the Earth, like the glass in a greenhouse. This makes the atmosphere warmer than if the heat was able to escape into space.

habitats The places where living things make their homes; the environments that they are adapted to survive in.

herbivores Animals that feed mainly on plants; plant-eaters.

humid Damp or moist.

mammals Animals that are warm-blooded and usually have hair on their skin, including humans and lions. Female mammals produce milk to feed their young.

marsupials Types of mammals whose young are born very underdeveloped and are carried around in a pouch by the mother for some time after they are born. Kangaroos and wombats are marsupials.

migrate To move from one place to another in search of better living conditions.

monsoon A wind that blows across southern Asia from around April to September, bringing heavy rain.

nutrients Another word for food – all the things needed for a balanced diet which provides energy and raw materials for growth and maintenance of the organism.

poachers People who illegally hunt animals, especially by trespassing.

porous Describes something that allows fluid to pass through it, or that has many tiny holes (pores) in it.

predators Animals that catch and eat other animals for food.

prey Animals that are caught and eaten by predators.

recycling Reusing waste materials.

scavenge To look for food discarded or left behind by others. Animals that feed on the leftover remains of another animal's meal are called scavengers.

species A group of living things with the same general appearance and behaviour, that can breed together to produce fertile offspring.

stampede The sudden, panicked rush of a herd of horses or cows, or a crowd of people, when frightened.

Index

animals, 4-5, 12-27
  ants, 24-25
  eagles, 15, 27
  hyraxes, 26-27
  insects, 13, 24-25
  kangaroos, 18-19
  lions, 20-21
  mongooses, 27
  ostriches, 15
  red-billed queleas, 15
  secretary birds, 15
  wallabies, 18-19
  weavers, 14
  wild dogs, 22-23
  wildebeest, 16-17

climate, 6-7
  dry season, 6
  monsoon zone, 6
  rainy season, 7

damage, 28-29
desertification, 29

fires, 10-11
flooding, 5
flowers, 8

grasses, 7, 8-9, 11

human origins, 28

kopjes, 26-27

soil, 8, 13

trees, 4, 5, 11, 24-25
  acacias, 24-25